COMPACT DISC PAGE AND BAND INFORMATION

Music Minus One

4057

Tenor Opera Arias with Orchestra

A NOTE ON THE ARIAS

The tenor voice in opera is of course a symbol of masculinity, and indeed often one of great determination. But unlike the more blatant *machismo* of the baritone or the basso, the tenor is also a symbol of poeticism, sincerity, sensitivity and longing. And in this selection of Italian arias, those qualities are ever-present. From Puccini's utterly sensitive portrayal of love's first blossom to Verdi's masterstrokes revealing the shame of a man unwittingly enjoying the fruits of his beloved's sacrifices, they demonstrate the wide variety of emotional and dramatic content in the vast tenor repertoire.

Puccini's *La Bohème* stands at the summit of Italian romantic opera, and it was his first truly successful work. Even though the earlier *Manon Lescaut* had in general been a success, it was not to withstand certain objections on a critical level which remain to this day. But with *Bohème* he created a synthesis of music and drama which seem to be as near to perfection as one can come. And in the aria **"Che gelida manina"** the young bohemian Rodolfo introduces himself to Mimi, who has knocked at his door looking for a light for her candle. As he takes her cold hand in his own, his tender song of his dreams of love is an appropriately magical introduction to her "Mi chiamano Mimi," and it is one of Rodolfo's most beautiful arias. In his orchestration, Puccini begins with gentle strings and a harp to underscore the delicacy of his love, his reaction to the equally delicate Mimi, then rises in intensity and thickness of sound as he becomes more impassioned and speaks to her of his dreams.

For his next opera, *Tosca*, Puccini dealt with heavier themes, namely the political climate of Rome at the dawn of the nineteenth century. He therefore gave the tenor part of Cavaradossi a less ethereal rôle than that of Rodolfo in *Bohème*, and the opera, being much more daring in musical construction than any of Puccini's previous works, had a harder time gaining initial recognition, but soon became accepted as the masterpiece of dramatic and musical power that it is. In **"Recondita armonia,"** which takes place early in the first act, again the tenor sings of love, but in this case this painter sings of the Madonna in his painting, and her resemblance to Floria Tosca, his mistress. Puccini gives this aria a complex orchestral backdrop and the tenor's line is bold and impassioned from start to finish.

Donizetti, in composing *L'Elisir d'Amore*, intended to create a successful *opéra comique* that would have lasting value, and that he did, succeeding admirably. In fact this is the first of his operas to hold a steady place in the repertoire, a status it has retained since its premiere in Milan on 12 May 1832. The memorable and justifiably famous aria **"Una furtiva lagrima"** in which Nemorino sings an impassioned song of his undying love for the heretofore uninterested Adina. The aria is sung against the backdrop of an arpeggiated harp and a beautiful woodwind accompaniment, in which Donizetti masterfully uses a minor key to echo the depths of Nemorino's longing. Donizetti's masterstroke in this opera was knowing that the purely comedic songs must be counterbalanced by arias of real emotional content, thereby lending the pathos necessary for a memorable and complete comedy.

Verdi's *Rigoletto* is the source of what is unequivocally one of the most famous of all tenor arias, **"La donna è mobile."** Based on Victor Hugo's scandalous play *Le roi s'amuse*, the opera prémiered 11 March 1851 in Venice, after being rejected twice by the Venetian censors. And though it was an incredible public success, it encountered more censorship problems as it traveled to other countries. Its story of debauchery, vendetta and extreme tragedy was of prime interest to Verdi but disgusting to most censorship bodies of the time. In this aria, the hunchback Rigoletto has lured the debauched Duke of Mantua, who covets his daughter, to a tavern and house of ill repute where he has arranged for his murder. The aria, which Verdi placed in the context of a simple but very catchy tune, is scored in an exaggerated, almost circus-like atmosphere and its sense of braggadocio is perfectly suited to the dissolute nature of the Duke and his attitude towards the female sex.

It is hard to believe that *La Traviata*, not only one of Verdi's greatest works but also one of the greatest in all Italian opera, was initially a disaster. It was composed under poor circumstances: Verdi worked simultaneously on this work and also on the very different *Il Trovatore*; he was unhappy with parts of Paive's libretto and was therefore constantly working through the process of rewrites; and he was saddled with a terrible opening night cast, including an obese soprano playing the role of the consumptive Marguerite. The laughter this engendered at the work's prémiere on 6 March 1854 combined with numerous other problems to make it a dismal failure. But restage it Verdi did, this time personally supervising the production, and on 6 May 1854, two months later to the day, the opera was performed again, this time to thunderous ovation and lasting popularity and respect.

Alfredo's recitativo **"Lunge da Lei"** and its accompanying aria **"De miei bollenti spiriti,"** which open Act Two, provide a perfect example of Verdi's dramatic command. In this scene, Alfredo has returned to the country house outside Paris, and has discovered that his beloved Violetta has been selling her possessions for his sake. And for this tale of the Lady of the Camellias, Verdi has kept the tenderness and passion readily apparent, but interwoven skilfully with the urgency of Rodolfo's shame. The recitativo is orchestrated with simple string accompaniment, and the aria itself is underscored simply with a triplet rhythm played by *pizzicato* strings, and clarinet, bassoon, and horn lend a soft, steady backdrop to his impassioned aria. And thus it is the voice that so singularly carries the weight of the aria, in a way only Verdi could master.

—Michael Norell

Puccini
La Bohème
"Che gelida manina"

Ma per for - tu - na è u-na not - te di lu - na,—— e qui la

lu - na l'ab - bia - mo vi - ci - na. A - spet - ti, si - gno - ri - na—— le di-

rò con due pa - ro - le chi son, chi son, e che fac - cio,

co - me—— vi - vo. Vuo - le? Chi

me - re e per ca-stel - li in a - ria,___ l'a-ni-ma ho mi - lio - na

ria. Ta - lor dal mio for - zie - re___ ru - ban tut-ti i gio -

iel - li due la-dri: gli oc-chi bel - li. V'en - trar con voi pur o - ra,

poco allargando
con anima

ed i miei so - gni u - sa - ti   e i bei so - gni mie - i

dolciss. molto rall.

to - sto si di - le - guar!_____ Ma il fur - to non m'ac-

a tempo

co - ra   poi - chè,_____ poi - chè v'ha pre - so

10

Ossia

stan - za la spe - ran - za!

stan - za la dol - ce spe - ran - za!

allarg. sempre dolcissimo

con anima stentando allarg.

Or che mi co-no-sce - te par-la-te vo - i. Deh! par-la-te. Chi sie - te?

rall.

Vi piac - cia dir!

MMO 4057

Puccini
Tosca
"Recondita armonia"

MMO 4057

te. bel _ ta _ dei gno _ ta,............

.......cin _ ta di chio_me bion _ _ de!...

Tu az_zur _ ro hai l'oc _ _ chio............

.......To_sca ha l'oc _ chio ne _ _ ro!

SAGR.

Scherza coi fanti e lascia stare i

Donizetti
L'Elisir d'Amore
"Una furtiva lagrima"

Nemorino

dolce

U - na fur - ti - va la-gri-ma ne - gl'oc-chi suoi spun - tò.

Quel - le fe - sto - se gio - va - ni in - vi - di - ar_ sem -

bro. Che più cer - can - do io vo'?

Che più cer - can - do io vo'? M'a - ma. Sì,

m'a - ma._ Lo ve - do, lo ve - do.

Un so - lo i - stan - te i pal - pi - ti del suo bel cor___ sen - tir! I miei so - spir con - fon - de - re per po - co a' suoi___ so - spir! I pal - pi - ti, i pal - pi - ti sen - tir, con - fon - de - re i miei co' suoi so -

*This alternate cadenza has become traditional.

Verdi
Rigoletto
"La donna è mobile"

La don-na è mo-bi-le qual piuma al ven-to, mu-ta d'ac-cen-to

E sempre mi-se-ro chi a lei s'af-fi da, chi le con - fi-da

mal cau-to il co - re! Pur mai non sen-te-si fe-li-ce ap-pie - no

chi su quel se - no non li-ba a - mo-re! La_donna è mo-bil

qual piuma al ven-to, mu-ta d'ac-cen-to e_di pen-sier,

Verdi
La Traviata
Scene and Aria: *"Lunge da lei"*

(depone il fucile)

le _ i per me non v'ha di _ let_to!..

a tempo

Vo _ la _ ron già tre lu _ ne dac _ chè la mia Vio_

_let_ta a_gi per me la _ sciò, do_vi_zie, o _ no_ri e le pom_po _ se

fe_ste, ov' a_gli omaggi av_vez _ za, ve_dea schia_vo cia _ scun di sua bel_

Verdi
La Traviata
"De' miei bollenti spiriti"

vi _ ve _ re   io   vo _ glio, io voglio a te   fe_

_del,   del _ l'u _ ni_ver_so im_me _ mo _ re   io

vi _ _ vo, io vi _ vo qua _ si, io vi_vo qua _ si in

ciel.   *Dal dì che dis_se:*   vi _ ve _ re io voglio a te   fe_

io. vi_vo quasi in ciel,... ah. sì, io vi_vo quasi in cie_lo, io vi_vo quasi in

ciel.

Music Minus One Vocal Recordings

SCHUBERT GERMAN LIEDER - High Voice, Volume 1
....MMO CD 4001
SCHUBERT GERMAN LIEDER - Low Voice, Volume 1
....MMO CD 4002
SCHUBERT GERMAN LIEDER - High Voice, Volume 2
....MMO CD 4003
SCHUBERT GERMAN LIEDER - Low Voice, Vol. 2
....MMO CD 4004
BRAHMS GERMAN LIEDER - High Voice.............MMO CD 4005
BRAHMS GERMAN LIEDER - Low Voice ....MMO CD 4006
EVERYBODY'S FAVORITE SONGS - High Voice, Vol. 1
....MMO CD 4007
EVERYBODY'S FAVORITE SONGS - Low Voice, Vol. 1 .
....MMO CD 4008
EVERYBODY'S FAVORITE SONGS - High Voice, Vol. 2
....MMO CD 4009
EVERYBODY'S FAVORITE SONGS - Low Voice, Vol. 2 .
....MMO CD 4010
17th/18th CENT. ITALIAN SONGS - High Voice, Vol. 1
....MMO CD 4011
17th/18th CENT. ITALIAN SONGS - Low Voice, Vol. 1
....MMO CD 4012
17th/18th CENT. ITALIAN SONGS - High Voice, Vol. 2 ..MMO CD 4013
17th/18th CENT. ITALIAN SONGS - Low Voice, Vol. 2 .....MMO CD 4014
FAMOUS SOPRANO ARIAS ....MMO CD 4015
FAMOUS MEZZO-SOPRANO ARIAS ....MMO CD 4016
FAMOUS TENOR ARIAS .... MMO CD 4017
FAMOUS BARITONE ARIAS ....MMO CD 4018
FAMOUS BASS ARIAS...MMO CD 4019
WOLF GERMAN LIEDER FOR HIGH VOICE ....MMO CD 4020
WOLF GERMAN LIEDER FOR LOW VOICE ....MMO CD 4021
STRAUSS GERMAN LIEDER FOR HIGH VOICE....MMO CD 4022
STRAUSS GERMAN LIEDER FOR LOW VOICE .....MMO CD 4023
SCHUMANN GERMAN LIEDER FOR HIGH VOICE ....MMO CD 4024
SCHUMANN GERMAN LIEDER FOR LOW VOICE ....MMO CD 4025
MOZART ARIAS FOR SOPRANO ....MMO CD 4026
VERDI ARIAS FOR SOPRANO ....MMO CD 4027
ITALIAN ARIAS FOR SOPRANO..........................MMO CD 4028
FRENCH ARIAS FOR SOPRANO..........................MMO CD 4029
ORATORIO ARIAS FOR SOPRANO ....MMO CD 4030
ORATORIO ARIAS FOR ALTO ....MMO CD 4031
ORATORIO ARIAS FOR TENOR ....MMO CD 4032
ORATORIO ARIAS FOR BASS ....MMO CD 4033
BEGINNING SOPRANO SOLOS Kate Hurney ....MMO CD 4041
INTERMEDIATE SOPRANO SOLOS Kate Hurney....MMO CD 4042
BEGINNING MEZZO SOPRANO SOLOS F. Kittelson ....MMO CD 4043
INTERMEDIATE MEZZO SOPRANO SOLOS F. Kittelson ....MMO CD 4044
ADVANCED MEZZO SOPRANO SOLOS F. Kittelson ....MMO CD 4045
BEGINNING CONTRALTO SOLOS Carline Ray ....MMO CD 4046
BEGINNING TENOR SOLOS George Shirley ....MMO CD 4047
INTERMEDIATE TENOR SOLOS George Shirley ......MMO CD 4048
ADVANCED TENOR SOLOS George Shirley ....MMO CD 4049
TWELVE CLASSIC VOCAL STANDARDS, VOL.1 .....MMO CD 4050
TWELVE CLASSIC VOCAL STANDARDS, VOL.2 .....MMO CD 4051
SOPRANO OPERA ARIAS WITH ORCHESTRA ....MMO CD 4052
PUCCINI ARIAS FOR SOPRANO WITH ORCHESTRA . ....MMO CD 4053
SOPRANO OPERA ARIAS WITH ORCHESTRA ....MMO CD 4054
VERDI ARIAS FOR MEZZO-SOPRANO WITH ORCHESTRA ....MMO CD 4055
BASS-BARITONE ARIAS WITH ORCHESTRA ....MMO CD 4056
TENOR OPERA ARIAS WITH ORCHESTRA ....MMO CD 4057
SOPRANO OPERA ARIAS WITH ORCHESTRA ....MMO CD 4058

Music Minus One Tenor

PUCCINI - La Bohème
Che gelida manina (Rodolfo)

PUCCINI - Tosca
Recondita armonia (Cavaradossi)

DONIZETTI - L'Elisir d'Amore
Una furtiva lagrima (Nemorino)

VERDI - Rigoletto
La donna è mobile (Duca)

VERDI - La Traviata scene and aria:
Lunge da Lei...
Dei miei bollenti spiriti (Alfredo)

Italian Tenor Arias
with Orchestra

MMO

4057

MMO Music Group • 50 Executive Boulevard, Elmsford, New York 10523, 1-(800) 669-7464
Website: www. minusone.com • E-mail: mmomus@aol.com